W9-BER-719

CCSS **Genre** Nonfiction

Essential Question

What do friends do together?

Friends Are Fun

by Liza Kendall

Friends are fun. You can run with a friend. Come on, let's go!

You can hop with a friend, too. Friends like to play.

Friends can help you.
They can help you ride
a bike.

They can help you make
a fort. It's fun to help
a friend.

Friends can share.
They can share a book.

They can share an apple, too. Friends like to share.

A friend can be big or little. Do you have big friends and little friends?

This friend has four legs!
A dog can be a very
good friend.

It is good to have friends.
Friends are fun. You can
do a lot with friends.

What can you do with
your friends?

Respond to Reading

Retell

Use your own words to retell details in *Friends Are Fun.*

Detail	Detail	Detail

Text Evidence

1. Look at page 3. What details tell what you can do with a friend? Key Details

2. Look at page 6. What can friends share? Key Details

3. How can you tell that *Friends Are Fun* is nonfiction? Genre

CCSS **Genre** Poetry

Compare Texts
Read about what these friends like to do together.

I Like to Play

With my friend Sam
I like to race.
We shoot our rockets
into space.

With my friend Ana
I like to run.
Playing soccer
is lots of fun.

With my friend Dan
I like to dig.
We make a castle,
tall and big.

Make Connections

Look at both selections. How do friends play together? Text to Text

Focus on
Social Studies

Purpose To find out what your friends do when they play

What to Do

Step 1 Draw a chart like this one.

My friends	Like to

Step 2 Ask your friends what they like to do when they play together.

Step 3 Write what your friends like to do. Tell your class.